THE A B C OF COMPASSIONATE COMMUNICATION

26 steps to improve your compassion and communication

SUE SILCOX

Author: Sue Silcox

ABN: 38632205746

Website: www.brainsparks.com.au

Email: sue@brainsparks.com.au

Facebook: Ageinganddementia

Copyright: © 2019 Brain Sparks Pty Ltd

Company: Brain Sparks Pty Ltd

First Published: 2019

The moral rights of the author have been asserted.

All rights reserved. This book may not be reproduced in whole or in part, stored, posted on the Internet, or transmitted in any form, or by any means whether electronically, mechanically, by photocopying, recording, or any other means, without permission from the author and publisher of the book.

Edited by: Sue Silcox

Printed and bound in Australia by: Westminster Printing

ISBN: 978-0-6485189-0-7

Dedication

I would like to dedicate this book to all those people who, on a daily basis, struggle to communicate their needs; who may live in a different reality; put up with pain or emotions they just cannot express themselves, sometimes even just to tell us they love us.

And to the memory of my grandmothers, one of whom couldn't be heard, and the other who had words and actions of great wisdom. In different ways each had a huge influence on my life.

Introduction

Awakenings, the 1990 film drama, based on the true story of a doctor working with catatonic patients affected by Encephalitis Lethargica, used a drug to rouse people from their sleep state, and bring them into the world that they had missed for perhaps thirty or forty years. Although they regressed to their catatonic state, they had an awareness of what it means to be alive and be able to touch, love, dance, sing.

Imagine what it would be like not to be able to communicate: isolated, lonely, uninformed, untouched, perhaps unloved. What would you miss? There are people in our communities who can no longer communicate. They deserve our understanding, our love and most of all, our compassion so that they do not have to live, like Sleeping Beauty, isolated and alone.

The ABC of Compassionate Communication will give you hints and ideas of how we can improve our communication with everyone, because which of us knows who among us are lost in their own silent world.

 This symbol in the margin lets you know that ideas you can try follow.

Contents

Dedication iii
Introduction v
Awareness 2
Brain 6
Connection 10
Dementia 14
Empowerment 18
Friendship 22
Gratitude 26
Happiness 30
Isolation 34
Journey 38
Kindness 42

Laughter	46
Memory	50
Non-verbal Communication	54
Opportunity	58
Person-centred Care	62
Quality of Life	66
Reactions	70
Stigma	74
Touch	78
Understanding	82
Value	86
Wellness	90
eXtraordinary	94
You	98
Zzzzzzzz – sleep	102
Not the End	107
Thank You	109
Biography	111
References	113
How Sue Can Help You	117

The ABC of Compassionate Communication

 is for

wareness

How aware are you, firstly of your own self?

Self-awareness helps us find our strengths and it also allows us to work out where we need to improve. Self-reflecting on situations can show us where we match up to our own expectations and values.

Working on your self-awareness brings benefits not only to you but to those around you. Thinking about how you reacted with others brings awareness to your connections with others and ultimately makes you happier.

At quiet moments during the day, or just before sleep, spend time reflecting on what you did, or what others did.

AWARENESS

But don't just think about yourself. Become aware of what others feel by putting yourself in their situation. Rather than getting cross and irritated by someone's slowness or inability to follow an instruction, think about reasons that could be happening to them. Take a moment to become aware that they might be lost or confused. Perhaps they can't find the words to describe what they want. This is when your awareness of feelings can help someone have a better day.

 When lying in bed or sitting in a chair, close your eyes and take yourself into your body. In this case you are going to imagine your hands, but you can (and should) try this with other parts of your body. Starting with the thumb, trace the outline of your open hand in your mind's eye as though you had a long pencil from your brain that can draw around your hand. Imagine how it feels: does it tickle as the pencil gets in between the fingers? Is your hand hot or cold? If it's hot, can you imagine it cold, or vice versa. What shape or size is it? Feel the veins and imagine the blood rushing through your hands. Imagine the connective tissue, like a net, stretching and relaxing as it encloses the tissues. Now imagine your hand touching someone else's hand. What is it conveying? How would you use it to calm someone down? To tell someone you were there? To get someone to stop a repetitive action? To tell someone you loved them?

The ABC of Compassionate Communication

Next time you go into a shop, go to the information desk. When someone comes to help you, just look at them blankly. Hold that for, say, 15 seconds (it will feel a long time) and then say "oh" and turn away. If possible have a friend watch the reaction from a distance.

The focused meditation will help increase your own awareness and the second activity will bring your awareness to how it feels not to be able to communicate.

 is for

Brain

As the control centre, our brain looks out for itself first and foremost, it seems compassion comes after our own needs. The safety instructions just before a plane takes off inform us that in the event of an emergency, you put on your own oxygen mask before looking after someone else. That's a bit like our brain on empathy! You can only help someone else if you have looked after yourself first.

Nevertheless, our brains empathise when we see or read of suffering. An article in a book written in 1952 by psychotherapist Joseph Weiss, MD, shows that we cope through the stress and distress then, once it is over, we cry. Just think of those happy endings in the movies that have us sitting in our seats while we get ourselves back under control!

Dr Weiss suggests that because potential danger and threat may have a direct effect on our safety, our emotions are kept in check. Once danger is passed, we relax and the emotion can be processed. You may know this as the fight or flight response.

The part of our brain that looks after our safety is the limbic system, in particular the amygdala. The limbic system interacts with our autonomic nervous system, which has different functions for either rest or danger.

It appears that brain activity relating to empathy involves many brain regions. In particular, mirror neurons found in the frontal lobes of the brain are thought to play a big part in empathy. When you watch someone who is suffering in some way, perhaps they are trying to get out of a chair or are in pain, the mirror neurons fire and play the scene in your own mind so that you experience the feelings.

Connectivity between a region of the brain where thinking about others lives (the temporoparietal junction), and the region that supports abstract thinking (inferior frontal gyrus) seems to be where empathy lies. Strong connections between these regions help us interpret nonverbal cues better, leading to how we relate to others.

Compassion can be taught and improved through meditation, especially a technique called 'loving kindness meditation'. When we meditate, the brain regions for emotions and feelings change considerably (Bergland, 2012).

 Click on http://cmtcenter.net/wp-content/uploads/2017/07/Weiss1952.pdf to a 15-minute loving-kindness meditation from Emma Seppala Science Director of Stanford University's Center for Compassion and Altruism Research and Education and author of "The Happiness Track."

There's an 8-minute Ted Talk entitled 'The neurons that shaped civilization - VS Ramachandran' that you may find interesting.

C is for

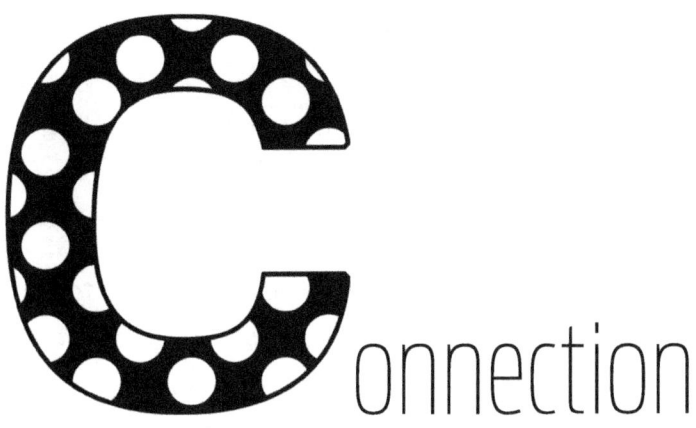
Connection

Connection is about relationships, which is why it is important in compassion. As well as the billions of neural connections within our brain, we connect person-to-person, with animals, plants and our environment. Furthermore, we can also have connections with inanimate things. You probably have at least one precious item that connects you to a memory, a person or place.

As we age or develop neurological or mental health conditions it can become more difficult to make and keep connections with friends and family. Feeling confused, alarmed by loud voices, not knowing what to say or how to join in give us the feeling of disconnect. This is how social isolation and loneliness can overtake us, even with a large social network, and unless we have an understanding care partner we may withdraw more and more.

Connection

Loneliness is a bigger risk factor to death than obesity and lonely people are more likely to be affected by pain and other health conditions. We may not see that someone is feeling lonely and isolated, making it more of a threat to health than we can realise.

It's easy to tell someone to join a club or go to the gym, but what can you do to help someone who is lonely? It is important to find ways to reconnect. For younger people, we need to get them to put down their phone and get off the computer. Older people are less likely to be doing that but there are many programs aimed at the senior (and older) community, often run by local councils. While exercise is enjoyable for many, others hate the idea but only think of it as pumping iron or running up a sweat!

 Go to your local library and see what groups are there. Talk to the librarian about finding information on something that interests you.

If you like gardening, join a gardening club.

Try a respite or day community centre. They have things for you to do, but more importantly, there are other people to talk to.

Join a group that offers different exercise, such as an aquarobics group, or Try Chi. If Ageless Grace® is in your area, join one of their classes to laugh, move and play.

The ABC of Compassionate Communication

If you are housebound, get back in touch with colleagues and friends and ask them to come and visit you. Once you find something that you like, you are more likely to find others.

 is for

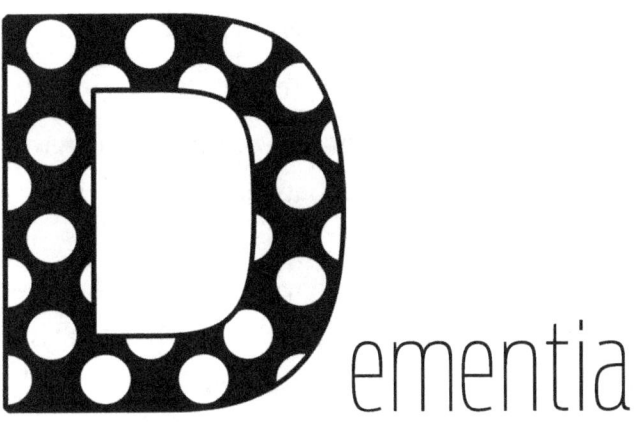ementia

Dementia is little understood across the world, but its impact is being felt in huge waves across the globe.

Dementia is the umbrella term for a large number of diseases seen as a progressive decline in function. Although you may think it is something that has only just been discovered, it has been around for centuries, but as many people died young, they would not have shown any symptoms. Currently, there is no cure for dementia although much effort is being put into both finding a cure and finding a way to prevent it in the first place.

At the moment, in Australia it is the leading cause of death for women and second highest for men. It's not a new phenomenon, but the global increase in ageing has meant that more people are being diagnosed, as it does affect people over 65 more than any other age group.

Although the tendency is for people to think "it's just that he's getting old" there is a difference between normal ageing and dementia. In normal ageing, we can still be functional, albeit slower of mind and body and perhaps a bit forgetful. But in dementia there may be vague indications that all is not as it should be. The people closest to the person, usually the family, may notice that the person is increasingly confused; they may have times when they are not aware of where they are, or their memory seems to be much worse than it used to be. If that person is behaving strangely, perhaps is showing anxiety then it is worth talking to a doctor who can ask you about what you are noticing.

Sometimes the problem may appear to be dementia that has come on through an infection, for example. Your doctor may prescribe something that will clear up the problem and things will go back to what is pretty close to normal.

Communicating with someone with dementia can sometimes be difficult, though that is not always the case. Put yourself in their shoes: perhaps they are feeling pain but cannot find the words to express it; imagine if you couldn't tell someone how you felt – you would probably be frustrated and may lash out in anger. A person living with dementia has to find different ways to

The ABC of Compassionate Communication

express themselves and you may find it embarrassing or irrational. That's when your compassion can help you both.

 There are many videos that explain dementia on the internet. This short video shows how you can connect with someone non-verbally.

Experts make dementia communication breakthrough.

You can find it at
https://www.youtube.com/watch?v=MpV7IhhOZ4Y

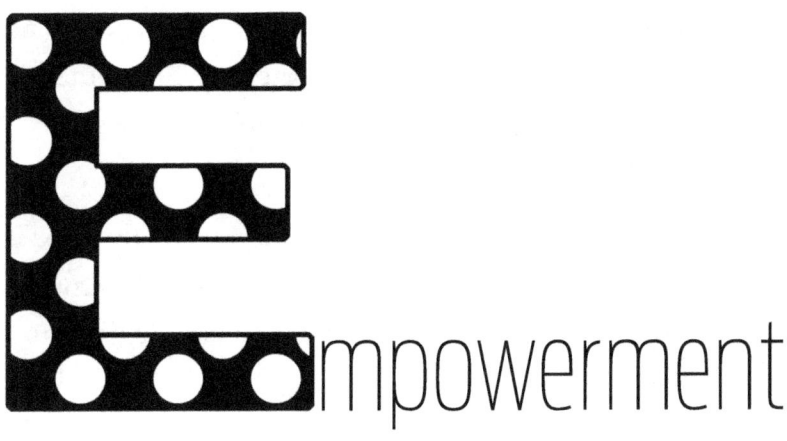
Empowerment

> *"Empowerment is about giving people the means to pursue the process of gaining freedom and power to do what you want or control what happens to you."*
> (Cambridge English Dictionary, amended by author).

Empowerment increases your motivation and desire to remove obstacles that people face in what they do.

Often people who are in care situations are not given the means to empower themselves. They may not realise this as they go about their tasks to the best of their ability. Empowering them can help them realise what they can do to improve not only their lives, but those they care for as well.

Empowerment

Empowerment means having relevant information. Knowing you need to understand dementia because you work in a dementia care unit but not having training or coaching to learn the subject, leads to frustration and inefficiency.

Empowerment means having the authority to do the job. If you have to constantly ask a supervisor or manager if you can do something that will help someone in your care, that is not empowerment. Is your voice heard?

Empowerment means being able to collaborate with others because your ideas are respected. Are you able to look for solutions to problems you encounter or are you told just to do it the same old way?

If you are feeling powerless in your work or your life, you can change it. Try some of the ideas.

 The first one is pretty simple. Change your use of the phrase "I can't" to "I can".

> Learn as much as you can. Learn about how you can improve your job. Learn about how other people do things. Learn where you can meet people who are in situations like yours. Learning will improve your situation and learning new things is good for your brain, too.

Take time out. Think about the situation and what you could do to improve it. Once you have thought up a solution you can tell someone. Be the change.

Concentrate on what you can control or change. You won't be able to do it all – well not all at once, anyway – so do the things that you can. Be empowered!

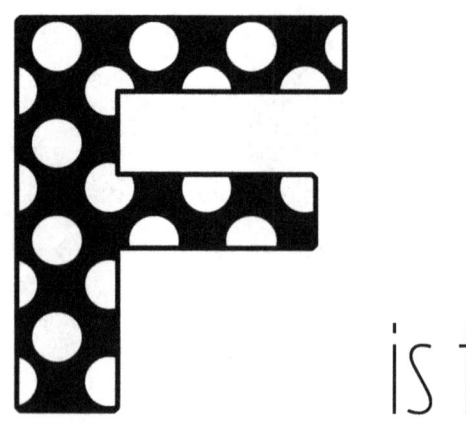 is for

riendship

Having a friend is having a relationship with someone with whom you have shared experiences, time, stories and done fun or interesting things together.

Think about your oldest friend, that is the friend you have known the longest. It may or may not be the person you share, or have shared, your life with. How do you feel when you think about them? How do you feel when they are going through difficult periods in their lives?

Having a friend extends our life expectancy and lessens the chances of disease. Friendships can release the neuropeptide, oxytocin, which helps us feel good and it lights up our brain.

FRIENDSHIP

For many people, their best friend is the person they share their life with and communication between them is probably mostly easy. I know that with my partner, we both start to say the same thing at the same time, which gives great feelings of connection. But, like all relationships, it's not all roses and we don't always see eye-to-eye, leading to a certain level of stress. It can feel like that when you have a falling out with a good friend. Hopefully, it gets better.

Good friendships sometimes need effort. Are you able to be there for your friend when times are tough for them? Are you able to listen and not cast judgement?

If you don't already, try these tips on keeping compassionate friendships:

If they are going through a tough time, offer your support and your ear.

 If it's something that they like to do, give them a hug, and when you've finished, give them another. You should know whether your friend likes a hug or not and, by checking the body language, you will be able to see what they need right now.

Sometimes your friend may be dealing with mental health issues. This is when you really need to be a compassionate communicator. Be there, or on the end of a phone, and encourage them to talk. Ask about their feelings and encourage them to get help if things look bad for them. You may even have to seek help for them yourself rather than risk them harming themselves.

Have fun. Talk about the things you've shared over your friendships. Agree to disagree sometimes.

All this makes for a strong, healthy friendship that will fill you both with happiness.

 is for

ratitude

What has been good for you in your life today? Perhaps it rained and you didn't have to water the plants. Or maybe the sun came out and made you go for a walk. Last week I was walking with my grandson when we came across a garden with roses. As he is only young and probably hasn't had the chance to smell too many roses, I lifted him up so we could enjoy the beautiful fragrance. Wow! Was that a gratitude moment – I was grateful that we were walking together as we don't live near; I was filled with gratitude that not only did I have the strength to lift him up, but also that my sense of smell had me enjoying the fragrance of the roses as well as the fragrance of clean hair. And I was filled with gratitude for the people who lived in that house and who cared for the roses.

Gratitude

Results from many pieces of research show that expressing gratitude gives us emotional benefits, making us more resilient, less envious and more content. It gives us social benefits too, making us kinder with deeper friendships and relationships. In terms of health and personality, its benefits are increased longevity and self-esteem, more optimism and much less likely to be driven by materialistic motives. It can even improve your career through improving your decision making, increasing productivity and satisfaction and better networks.

Which man would you be?

> *"Once times were tough. Two men--both poor farmers--were walking down a country lane and met their Rabbi. "How is it for you?" the Rabbi asked the first man. "Lousy," he grumbled, bemoaning his lot and lack. "Terrible, hard, awful. Not worth getting out of bed for. Life is lousy." Now, God was eavesdropping on this conversation. "Lousy?" the Almighty thought. "You think your life is lousy now, you ungrateful lout? I'll show you what lousy is." Then, the Rabbi turned to the second man. "And you, my friend?" "Ah, Rabbi--life is good. God is so gracious, so generous. Each morning when I awaken, I'm so grateful for another day, for I know, rain or shine, it will unfold in wonder and blessings too bountiful to count. Life is*

The ABC of Compassionate Communication

so good." God smiled as the second man's thanksgiving soared upwards until it became one with the harmony of the heavenly hosts. Then the Almighty roared with delighted laughter. "Good? You think your life is good now? I'll show you what good is!"

The Simple Abundance Journal of Gratitude.
Sarah Ban Breathnach

 If you don't already have one, get yourself a book and every day write three things that have made you grateful.

appiness

A friend of mine once asked me to describe myself in one word. After a moment's thought I replied "Happy". I quite often think about the question and how whether that response still holds true, and I can honestly say that, for me, it is. And I am truly grateful that it is!

Why is happiness so important to our level of compassion and our engagement with people? Well, it makes us healthier, more productive, improves your relationships and can improve your wealth. That signifies a reason to find happiness while also accepting that you don't have to be happy all the time, and that there will be times when you feel sad or have issues to deal with.

HAPPINESS

Happiness is known to play a role in our health as happy people are likely to spend more time with friends, to exercise, to sleep better, to socialise more and have a healthier diet.

Our brain is involved in our happiness through those regions that deal with our emotions. The frontal lobe is a major part of our brain involved in emotional expression, memory, language, problem solving and sexual behaviour. Another part, the thalamus, has a role in the emotional response.

It is the neurotransmitters, the brain's chemical messengers, and the hormones that influence how we feel. Neurotransmitters transmit signals between neurons or between nerve cells and muscle cells. Dopamine is one that makes us motivated and aids our concentration; it can make us feel blissful and euphoric. You may know dopamine as the "feel good" hormone. Serotonin is another which contributes to our happiness and well-being. Oxytocin is a hormone that plays a big role in childbirth and lactation and is known as the "cuddle hormone or "love hormone". You may also have heard how exercise releases endorphins and help make you feel good. Endorphins can be thought of as boosting happiness, but they also help relieve pain.

 You can make yourself feel happy. Why not give them a go?

Even though you may not be feeling like it, SMILE! Your brain will release those neurotransmitters.

Dance is a great form of exercise to promote happiness as it involves emotional expression, too. If you dance with someone else you are also connecting, but so is putting on music at home and dancing to it. If it makes you laugh, even better!

 is for

solation

Many people who care for someone at home cope with isolation and loneliness, as can their care recipient.

Feeling isolated or lonely are two similar emotions with slightly different origins. Loneliness is when you feel sad or distressed because you are not connected with the people or the world around you. Ironically, loneliness can be felt when you are surrounded by others, as you would have read under 'C is for Connection'.

Isolation is different because you feel separated from other people or from the environment. People in remote areas can often feel isolated because of the distances they have to travel. Even not

ISOLATION

being able to contact someone because they are far away can have you feel isolated.

The effects of loneliness and isolation include your physical, mental and social health. If you are isolated or lonely, you have a lot of time to think about yourself and dwell on aches and pains (real or imagined). This can then lead to anxiety and depression. Many people suffer panic attacks as they imagine all sorts of things.

Poor quality sleep, low energy, lack of desire to care for yourself as you care for someone else can lead to greater unhappiness and feeling helpless.

To counter these feelings, many people turn to alcohol or drugs to ease the pain, all of which mask the problem without being able to solve it.

Isolation and loneliness are real, and you may need to ask for help in order to cope. Physical isolation is not easy to change but perhaps you can find opportunities to get in touch with other people in your vicinity. Unfortunately, Australia's huge size with poor infrastructure in remote areas can make it feel much more difficult to do this. But persevere.

 If you live in a remote location, you may relate much better with your environment. Perhaps you have a beautiful spot that you love to visit. If not, why not find a photograph or image of this spot and spend some time there every day, imagining yourself in the picture. I have a friend in Wales who spends five to ten minutes each day, with her eyes closed, imaging beautiful places that she could be. She finds it very helpful.

Technology can be helpful in letting you keep in touch with people far away. If you live in a remote location your communication channels may not be as fast as those closer to metropolitan areas, but keeping in touch via Skype or Facetime, sending emails and photos can go some way to relieving the loneliness of isolation.

 is for

Journey

Life is certainly a journey. We set out as young adults, excited to be on our way. Enthusiasm and excitement often accompany the young as they take on the adult world.

Like any journey, there are many wonderful times. Seeing and experiencing different parts of the country or the globe can have us feeling euphoric and glad to be alive. We make lots of friends, often from many nationalities and in my case, many of these friends are still part of my life.

There are difficulties too. Unexpected obstacles can get in our way. Perhaps we lose our wallet or miss a connection. Then there are the parts that are uphill and that see us struggle through them. The journey often changes, too, either because we choose the change ourselves, or else the choice is taken from us.

Parts of those journeys will remain in our mind and in our memory. If we have shared that journey with someone else, we can relive them as we talk and laugh about them, look at the photos or the, sometimes tacky, mementos we brought back!

Sometimes parts of the journey have been sad, and when we remember them can make us feel sorry for ourselves. But sadness will pass. Sadness is the price we pay for living and when it is over the memories can be shared and talked about.

Journeying with someone you are no longer able to communicate with effectively can be sad but there are also times when you can still laugh together or comfort each other in some way. This is when something like Compassionate Touch® will connect you without the need for words. Those are the times to hold onto in this part of your journey. Remembering the good times will help get you through the obstacles and come out the other side.

 Be kind to yourself. You are doing a great job, even though there are probably many times when you don't feel as though you deserve it. You could take some time out and read that book that's been waiting for you. If you really can't be away from the person you are caring for, read it out loud to them! They will enjoy the close connection with you.

Stay positive. It will get better, perhaps not today, or this week or even this year, but it will improve. A gratitude journal helps or finding a daily affirmation. I find Kate Knapp's Twigseeds series to be a great way to lift my spirits.

Kindness

Who is the kindest person you know? What makes them that way? Do you think you are kind? Can anyone be kind all the time? What, exactly, is kindness?

There are a number of words to describe kindness, including friendly, helpful, generous and considerate. Perhaps you can find some more. It seems that people who show kindness experience more happiness in their own lives, which is a recurring theme through this book!

Kindness can come from a feeling of "well, if I do this act of kindness, I will get this reward in turn". Scientists call this 'strategic kindness' as you are using it to get something out of it. Then there is the altruistic kindness, where you do something

KINDNESS

without any expectation of reward or action, other than feeling good.

One lady at a dementia care unit I go to always tells me I am an angel, as I do things for her, such as give her the meal, take her a drink or play cards with her. Freely given, it takes no effort on my part and the reward for me is having that compassionate communication with her.

For many people who care they give freely. They share their love and their compassion. Often they may not get any reward and indeed, can be chastised by the person they are caring for who may have lost their capacity to be kind themselves.

The life of a caregiver can be very challenging and lonely. They may yearn for someone to show some kindness to them. That is something we can all do by showing acts of kindness to anyone who needs it. The dollar coin given to someone who needs it for the bus can make their day special. You may quickly forget the cup of coffee you bought for someone standing behind you in the queue but for them it may just bring a shine to their day and may precipitate an act of kindness to someone else.

 Get onto the Australian Kindness Movement website and take a look at some of the 'Kind Things to Do' or read 'Acts of Kindness'. I think you will be glad you did.

The ABC of Compassionate Communication

The following came from the kindness calendars available from Random Acts of Kindness website:

- Make an effort to start every conversation you have today on a positive note.

- "Accidentally" drop a dollar to make a stranger feel lucky.

- Look in the mirror & point out 10 things you like about your body.

Laughter

Is laughter the same as happiness? It certainly gives us feelings of happiness but we can be happy without laughing.

Laughter is good for our brain because it improves our memory, it reduces stress hormones, such as cortisol and reduces blood pressure. It relaxes us and improves mood. When we laugh with others it improves the social bonds we share.

It's not only the brain that laughter is good for. It is good for your body as the laughter causes contractions of your internal organs – like having an internal massage. The expulsion of air from your lungs is followed by deep intakes of breath and the noises of laughter create vibration through our internal organs, including the kidneys and the abdomen.

LAUGHTER

But what if you don't have anything to laugh at? It doesn't matter. Although you can laugh spontaneously at a joke, you can laugh for no reason. Why don't you just try it – start with a chuckle, like a baby and gradually increase the sound your laughter makes and the depth of the breath. You may have to force it, to start off with but quickly you will find your torso shakes and next thing you know, you are laughing at yourself! This is good to do with a partner, too. One person starts and very soon the other person is laughing too, which increases your laughter!

> *"Believe it or not, having a really hearty chuckle can help too [your health]. This is because laughing gets the diaphragm moving and this plays a vital part in moving blood around the body."*
>
> Dr Andrea Nelson, University of Leeds School of Healthcare

 Find a Laughter Yoga club in your local area. You will join in with others and laugh your way through gentle exercise that will make you feel good.

Find an Ageless Grace® class near you and let the music, the playfulness, the memories and images make you laugh while you move your body in an organic, functional way.

The ABC of Compassionate Communication

Stand in front of a mirror and look at your face. Then, start smiling at yourself in different ways. Smile as though you are shy; or confused. Smile as though you are about to meet someone famous. Once you've done that start to laugh. Take in a deep breath and let it out with guffaw and feel your belly wobble. Now titter as though you were the mouse who learned to laugh. Keep on laughing until you start to feel it coming naturally. Try it with someone else and make sure you have fun.

 is for

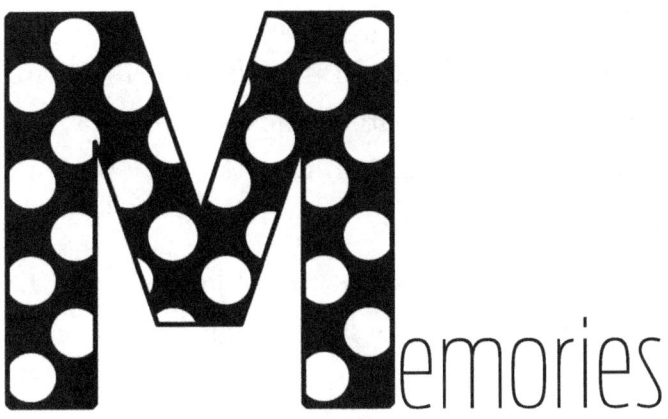Memories

This article first appeared on the Ageless Grace® Australia website as a blog.

I love how my memory works, and in case it loses some of my most treasured memories, I am saving them now to share later. Here's how I'm doing it.

How is your memory? Mine certainly isn't as sharp as it used to be in that I can't always find that word or remember where I left my glasses, but I still love and appreciate my memory for the amazing things it can do.

I like to listen to songs that I listened to as a child or young person. For example, at school in Wales we sang two hymns each day at assembly and on the rare occasions I hear one of them –

MEMORIES

last time was at a Royal wedding, – not only can I sing many of the words still, I can see myself back in the school hall, wearing the school uniform and standing with friends. It's probably one of the reasons I enjoy Ageless Grace® as much as I do as it becomes music therapy for me.

Reminiscences, such as these, bring a lot of joy and can help us tell stories that we would often not have the time or the words to share, especially if our present world is making less sense.

As I am getting older, I am taking photographs of the precious memories I have scattered around me in my house: the big bowl that was a wedding present that's been part of my life for all the years of my marriage; then there's the little gifts that bring back memories of places I've visited or family members. All those memories and scientists believe that this strengthens my memories as I recall them

Now that my parents are no longer with me, I have lots of questions I wish I had asked them, so I'm making my own life storybook that my family will be able to share with me as I get older but will also give them memories that they can pass on.

 This is something you can do for yourself and your loved ones. Keep your memories!

Meditation improves our memory because it slows down the brain activity. You can go to meditation classes or you

can find a quiet place each day and sit in stillness. Every time some thought comes into your head, let it go.

Berries, in particular blueberries, have been known to improve memory. They are high in flavonoids, which are thought to strengthen the connections in the brain. The herb, Rosemary, has been found to boost memory, reduce anxiety and depression, and improve sleep quality

 is for

on-verbal communication

Recently I was communicating with someone who was unable to express himself because he no longer has the ability to speak clearly. His level of frustration was evident through his gestures and body language as we tried to understand each other.

Communication relies on only between 10 and 20 percent of what we say, with tone of voice, or intonation, making up another 30 to 40 percent. Body language and gestures make up the remaining component of communication. This is what he and I were using to find common ground. Of course, there

Non-verbal Communication

was miscommunication, and I was interpreting what he was attempting to convey through my own experiences.

Fortunately, I had the time to spend with him. Imagine how difficult it is when you are in a caring role with several people you need to look after, or even just caring for the same person each and every day.

I am not sure how accurate our transmission was. What I do know is that without our attempts he would have continued to show anxiety and anger and been a danger maybe to himself or to others. By being able to spend that time with him, he became calmer and less agitated and as he become calmer, so did I.

It appears that communication in a dog's brain works in a similar way to ours, that is, dogs process the words they hear in the left side of the brain, and intonation in the right. Dogs appear to be able to distinguish words of praise used enthusiastically compared with those same words said in a lacklustre manner. What's more, enthusiastic praise lights up the reward centre in their brain. As we know that words play a small part in our communication, we need to adjust our communicate methods to make someone feel good. Body language and tone are vital.

Next time, when someone you know is having difficulty communicating, take the time to work with their body language

The ABC of Compassionate Communication

and remember that your intonation and gestures are much more likely to be what they remember of the encounter.

 Use good eye contact when speaking with someone else. You don't know if they have communication issues.

Use a calm, clear tone of voice and don't get agitated. Your body and voice will give it away.

 is for

Opportunities

We can go through life blindly or we can look for opportunities to help people as we go. Sometimes we have no choice, and we are cast into the role of care by nature of our relationships.

The opportunities I am thinking about are those that come our way on a daily basis, often like simple acts of kindness but sometimes through the people and circumstances that we come across.

Imagine this: You are in the local shopping centre and you see a small boy sitting on a bench crying. You can leave him be, or you could approach him and see if he is alright. In the current state of our society many of us tend not to interfere. There could

Opportunities

be a very good reason why he is there on his own, but he could be in danger from someone who may not be as compassionate as you. What do you think is the compassionate response?

1. You go towards him and ask him in a loud voice if he is OK and if he needs any help.

2. You go towards him, bend down so he can look you in the eyes when he is ready, and ask if he needs help.

3. You contact the Centre and tell them there is a boy crying outside a particular shop.

You are the only person who can decide what you would do, and you need to consider the course of action that could follow. Could your tone of voice make a difference? What about body language? Because you have no connection with this child and could be accused of interfering with a child are you better to let the Centre deal with it?

Every day we may encounter opportunities to help someone. The decision is yours.

The ABC of Compassionate Communication

 Consider your answers to these questions.

Should I give money to someone I meet on the street who asks me for money?

Should I report the shouting and screaming coming from a house in my street?

 is for

erson Centred Care

There are many ideas about how people with dementia or disability are cared for, one of them being that the person is at the centre of care and their communication needs are what we want to meet.

Rather like 'O is for Opportunity' we all have a chance to consider the response we will take, but for the person who is being cared for, their choice is often taken away. For reasons we think best, we take away items that may become a danger to them and then we don't replace them with something safer.

Person Centred Care

Whilst we are considering their safety, we are actually taking away their rights. Person centred care is not about allowing them to do what they want but is about giving them safe, meaningful options. Perhaps for the person who wants to go out into the garden they can have an indoor garden. If they want to help with the cooking, ingredients could be prepared beforehand so that all that is required is mixing.

These are two very simple examples and anyone who has to look after someone who has a disability or has dementia will have many more examples to relate. But put yourself in the care recipient's shoes. Often, the demands of family or of other residents means that they are left to their own devices for some time. Their concept of reality has changed and what we know and consider as rational actions are not for them.

By thinking and remembering the person being cared for – what they liked to do, or the responsible job they had, or the hobbies they followed – we can think more compassionately about what they are facing. If they act confused, it's not to pay you back. They are feeling confused. If they get angry, they are angry but not with you, rather the situation they find themselves in.

 If the person you are caring for is a family member you have the chance to communicate through the items in the house that belong to them, such as the old photos or books.

The ABC of Compassionate Communication

Residential homes are finding some people are enjoying using an iPad to listen to music they loved. Make it simple for them to operate and software companies have accessibility options to make it easier for them.

Consider using assistive technology. Is there a phone with large buttons and speed dial that can be used so that they can talk to someone?

Thinking outside the square helps when you are caring for someone with memory problems.

 is for

Quality of Life

Quality of life is the general wellbeing of individuals or societies. It will include factors such as health, communication, wellbeing, education, employment, safety, the environment and whether we feel we are valued. If we are able to provide a high quality of care, then quality of life will be improved.

For someone with dementia (also true for other disabilities) quality of care involves being able to interact in some way; to be engaged with caregivers and others, and to have opportunity for conversation. Of course, the amount of involvement in these tasks is dependent on their cognitive and physical function at the time, but if the interaction is relevant the individual is much more likely to take part.

Quality of Life

One way we can engage people is by getting them to do those things that they used to do. My grandmother always liked to go to the railway station! She talked about being taken there when she was in a wheelchair. Her disabilities were physical and in her later years progress in transport had been made, so her trips to the station ended up going by car. Ironically, my grandfather liked to take a walk to the cemetery on a Sunday afternoon. It was probably the closest green area around their house. Continuing those visits as they both aged and became infirm would have brought back many memories of earlier days.

Quality of life depends on other factors, too. For example, living conditions and leisure and social interactions. How do you measure quality of life? Measures have been in place around health aspects, such as depression, physical function, socialisation and emotional functioning. The measures are different from the more traditional medical measures, such as X-rays and other imaging techniques, blood tests, and clinical tests. Being able to assess for the quality of life measures makes a more rounded view of the person being assessed.

While mainly thinking about the person being cared for, we need to think about the quality of life of the caregiver. There are some ideas below to see how you rate and also to …

 You can check your wellbeing in the Australian Centre on Quality of Life

Engage with the person or people you care for that will help you talk about times past and share happy memories

Put on music from the care recipient's era and dance with them, either upright in a chair, or even in a bed. Movement stimulates the brain.

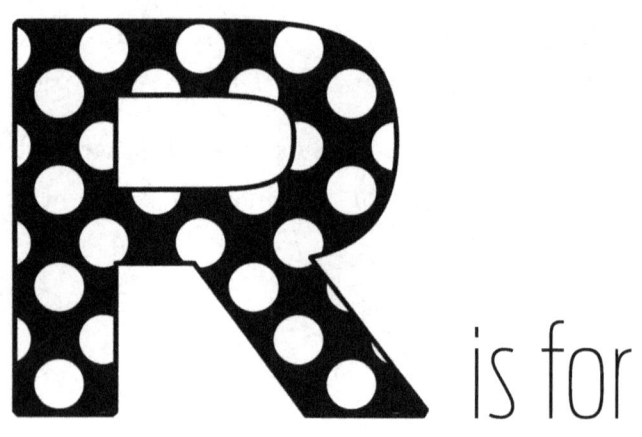 is for

Reacting

When caring for someone with dementia or disability they are often experiencing things going on in their body and brain that they can't explain, maybe don't even recognise. When the caregiver has to give some level of care, the individual may lash out, be unresponsive or shout. Sometimes their distress is shown in physical ways such as walking endlessly around the house or the facility. Sometimes their distress shows up as anxiety.

Where does the distress come from? In your caring role you made sure they are fed, they are showered and dressed, they have been put somewhere safely where they can watch the household and you think you have time to go and do something yourself. Perhaps your care recipient lives on their own and you are going to collect them to take them to the doctor or to the shops. You feel as though you are 100 percent there for them. And you are. However, something is not right in their world.

People with dementia or autism are likely to be adversely affected by their senses. Sitting in the living room with children running around, the washing machine going on in the background and you shouting at the dog can be noisy and distressing. How would you react? Having to take your clothes off (or have them taken off) and be taken into the shower while someone watches or helps them can be humiliating. How would you react? It is painful when you urinate, but you don't know why. How would you react?

The reality for people with dementia is often not the same as ours. Many of them talk about waiting for their mother or father or somebody from their past. When they are ignored or told that their mother or father are no longer with them, they are confused because those people are real in their memories at that time. How do you react when somebody tells you that what you believe is wrong, even though you had proof of it a few minutes ago?

Important, too, is the caregiver who is having to deal with potential abuse from the person they are caring for. Try to understand where the reaction has come from – why Mum is behaving like that. You need to look after yourself, too. Many of the tips in this book may help. If not, talk to someone; join a Facebook group for caregivers; get someone to give you a break so you can connect to nature. Express your emotion, too, but within a safe framework such as a support group.

 Express your negative emotions in a diary. No-one ever needs to see it but it allows you to vent.

Avoid reacting in a similar way.

Act and communicate compassionately with the person in your care.

 is for

Stigma

Social exclusion; discriminating or demeaning words or looks; denied entry into public places; made to feel shameful or humiliated because of an illness or disease; denied work because of a disability. It makes me very angry.

What one group of individuals finds hilarious – the name calling, physical or mental abuse and denial of rights – shames or humiliates the target group or individual and often, filled with despair.

Consider the person with epilepsy who is not given a job well within their capabilities but is discriminated against by a potential employer. Or the person with dementia that people label as 'stupid' or 'insane'.

Stigma

Apart from the name calling and being made to feel different, what possible other effects happen to those experiencing stigma? One effect is social isolation, no-one to share thoughts, hopes and ideas with. Another is to experience abuse or violence as well as loneliness.

Why do people stigmatise and discriminate against people with mental and physical disability? We already know that the human spirit inherently shows kindness, empathy and compassion so it must have something to do with prevailing family and society attitudes, peer pressure and lack of knowledge.

Look for opportunities to experience how you would feel if you had dementia. The Dementia Live® experience will not only take you through how it would feel, but you explore communication and care suggestions, too. You can read more about this research-based program on the Brain Sparks website.

I want to change stigmatisation. I hope you join my crusade!

 If you think you or someone close to you is being stigmatised, report it.

If you see someone being discriminated against, report it.

If you something in the media that stigmatises disability, report it.

Check out your own feelings to dementia and disability. Become a compassionate communicator.

The <u>SANE</u> website has fact sheets and guides about stigma and discrimination

 is for

ouch

Touch is a vital sense for our survival. Many people remember the neglected children in Romania's state-run orphanages. Without stimulation or comfort, children were often abused, left unattended due to high numbers of children to any one caregiver. Arising from political intervention due to falling birth rate the dictator, Ceausescu, initiated population policies that included banning abortion; a tax on childlessness; lowering the age at which people could marry and giving medals to mothers with the largest number of children. Unfortunately, he believed that the state would do a better job of parenting and many people were persuaded to give up their children to care.

Touch-deprived children are likely to die. Their development is affected by lack of touch. We have touch sensors all over our body, sensing pressure, vibration, temperature and pain. More of them are in some parts of the body, such as hands, tongue, lips, sexual organs, while other regions have only a few. Touch-deprived people are likely to die sooner.

Touch is important in bonding and communicating as well as providing physical and emotional support through life. There are several different types of touch, here are just three of them.

- We touch each other in greeting – a slap on the back; a handshake; a hug.

- We touch when we help someone, for example when you help someone out of a chair, attend a medical appointment or just want to point something out to someone.

- Importantly, we touch for emotional expression. We touch someone because we want to share a moment with them. We touch someone with our eyes when we look at them.

Older people, those with dementia or disability often aren't touched because we don't like to do it or because we don't think about.

Compassionate Touch® is an research-based intervention that may reduce the need for psychotropic medication. Easy to learn,

The ABC of Compassionate Communication

it is kind to both caregiver and care recipient. You can find out more about it on the Brain Sparks website.

 In your daily life, note the differences between how you touch your family members or people in your care. What type of touch do you use mainly.

One of the kindest things you can do for yourself is to touch your body and sense the different qualities of the touch.

 is for

Understanding

Pam Brandon, creator of the Dementia Live® and Compassionate Touch® training programs, writes that it is frightening to care for someone we don't understand. Both these programs teach caregivers and communities a deep understanding of dementia, its impact on the person with dementia as well as their families and provide ways to improve care practices. You can read more about these programs on the Brain Sparks website.

When we looked at stigmatisation and discrimination we learnt that we can improve this is by increasing our understanding and empathy for the people in our communities or those we care for.

Understanding

Before you can understand what someone else is going through you really need to understand yourself. By understanding what makes you "tick", what someone can say to hurt you, what it might feel like to be ostracised, how you feel when you are angry, happy, sad or any other emotion, you are starting to understand yourself.

Once you are aware of your own emotions (which is part of the Dementia Live® experience), you can start to think about others' views of the world. Is the view of a caregiver different from that of the care recipient? Is the view of the child different from that of the parent? You can start to think about why people do things that affect your life, for example, why did the car in front cut you off? Or what a boring hour you just spent learning all about fly fishing. What was the other person's reason for telling you?

What about other ways of looking at our understanding? People-watching is a great way to learn about understanding and empathy. It's important when talking with friends to notice their body language. If they're excited and you can recognise that, you will respond in a supportive manner. If they look as though they are feeling low or quieter than normal, your response is likely to be different. But caution, if you are responding to the reaction of someone with dementia you probably need to diffuse the situation, so try not to reflect their emotions if it is likely to make the situation worse.

The ABC of Compassionate Communication

 Next time you get angry, ask yourself what or who made you feel angry. Makeup a story would make you understand better what could have happened or what someone else had done to upset you.

Next time you people-watch check out their emotions. Enjoy telling yourself a story of why some of them look interested and some of them don't. Not only does it help your empathy, you can have great fun as you imagine funny scenarios!

 is for

# Value

One of my beliefs in life is that **Everyone has Value**.

A person's value is based around their own unique perspective, built up around the life they have lived and the things that affect them. It is also based on their physical and mental wellness and their ability to function.

Value is one the fundamentals around person-centered care. By this I mean that we maintain someone's dignity and respect through the acceptance of their decline or disability, realising that they can still perform actions that express their remaining, or innate, abilities. By considering value, we can turn Disability into disAbility and look for things that can be done, providing a stimulating environment for the person with dementia.

VALUE

Consider a family living at home with Grandad, who has Alzheimer's disease. Mum and Dad both work and share the care; the children both work but spend time with Grandad, as they love him. He likes to play cards but has forgotten many of the rules, so he "cheats". Or makes them up as he goes along. The young adults play cards with him and the value he brings to their time spent together is one of surprise as no one knows the rules from game to game! The children will have a lasting memory of the loving person he was and the laughter they shared. Compassionate communication respects individuals' values.

Aged care facilities that use Montessori Dementia as a model of care use meaningful activities to engage people. It can be a staged approach, with steps broken down into achievable actions. In this way, people who apparently were unable to do anything can achieve skills that their family and carers thought were forgotten.

 If caring for someone at home, get them to help you with a few small steps. Make it achievable for them.

> Help them lay the table. You can buy (or make) mats that have the knives, forks and spoons printed on them. If everything is ready they can use the mat as a template and help you with a job.
>
> Let them fold some of the clothes for you. It can be simple to do but rewarding for them to feel they are helping.

Let them help you sweep the floor, or arrange the flowers, or water the plants. These activities have meaning and acknowledge their value.

 is for

Wellness

Wellness is not just about our physical health and nutrition or about whether we exercise or not, though all these are important. There are other factors to wellness including, but not limited to, emotional, spiritual and environmental.

Wellness is important to quality of life so that, at whatever stage of life we are, we want to reduce stress, reduce illness and engage with others. It is the state of living a healthy lifestyle rather than health as a condition that you find yourself in, according to whichever illness or disease you may have. This means that you can be in poor health, but by looking after your emotional, mental and social state you can have wellness, which can lead to better health.

Wellness

The difference is simply explained like this. We cannot always choose the health we have. For example, you may have type I diabetes or have a genetic heart condition. You cannot change this. However, the choices you make around your health are wellness choices. You may choose to eat healthy foods, get annual checkups and do regular exercise. These lifestyle choices can perhaps help you to remain healthy for as long as possible.

Some of the wellness choices you can make include the following:

 Drink water first thing in the morning. It rehydrates you and flushes out toxins. Drink water throughout the day.

Get down onto the floor and then back up again as often as you can for one minute. It will pump oxygen into your lungs. It will open and close your joints and get your muscles moving. If you get used to getting onto the floor, if you fall down (I hope not), you know where you are and that you can get up.

Get some fresh air. It's good for your lungs, it's good for your circulation, it's good for your mental and emotional wellbeing. Taking a walk relieves stress.

Play music that you enjoy. It can revive memories and reduce stress levels. It makes you happy and may get you dancing and moving.

Challenge yourself. Try something new nearly every day. It may be driving a different way to the shops. Or walking on tiptoes through the house, which will help strengthen your legs and ankles – be careful not to fall down.

Eat more fruit and vegetables. They are good for you. Their different colours can make for a more interesting meal, as well as providing different nutrients. Try a rainbow salad or traffic light vegetables.

 is for

eXtraordinary

Many ordinary people are extraordinary. Many ordinary carers show extraordinary care. What makes someone extraordinary? Is it because no one else will do the job, or because they do it extremely well or is it because they have special qualities that go that extra step?

Extraordinary people are authentic, that is, they are genuine. They speak the truth about themselves, to themselves and to others. Being authentic is showing up as who you are, "warts and all", as the expression goes.

Extraordinary people make others feel special. They open doors for other people to come through. They say "thank you". They laugh at life yet care about others. They help to ease the pain that others feel. You can read another 120 things that make people special at 126 ways to be extraordinary from https://www.success.com/126-ways-to-be-extraordinary/ How extraordinary would you be if you found that in 126 days (or weeks) you had mastered all the suggestions in the list. I think you would be extraordinary just for trying.

Volunteers are extraordinary people. They are ordinary people doing extraordinary things for people they do not know. They do it because they choose to. Nobody has asked them to do it but often they see a need and want to help. Volunteers get back from the people they interact with as much, if not more than they put in.

Community Connections Inc tell stories about extraordinary people in their annual report. These heartwarming stories come from ordinary people who are passionate about care and helping others and even themselves. These two extracts are from the first people in the report. It's worth reading more about extraordinary people.

> **Wayne Silvia**: *Over the years, staff and clients have experienced his generosity in a variety of ways. He gives them free tickets to events, brings them gift cards to enjoy and takes staff out for lunch.*
>
> **Elaine Pieknik**: *Elaine is a clear example that hard work and determination can result in positive change*

and personal growth. In her continual quest for independence, she has progressed from the traditional day program into more advanced life skills training. Elaine has blossomed into a self-confident person with a ready smile and eagerness to learn new skills.

Look out for the extraordinary people in your life who make your life easier. Remember to thank them – it's the start of making you extraordinary!

 is for

Whether you are extraordinary or not, you are irreplaceable. How many people count on you? What would happen if you became sick or injured – how many people would be affected then?

Carer burnout is one of the effects of caring for people with dementia or disability. If you are suffering from carer burnout, you become physically and emotionally exhausted because of long exposure to the stresses of care. Your self-esteem may be low because of the emotional demands of your role and you may very well feel undervalued and taken for granted.

Signs of carer burnout include physical exhaustion which may be accompanied by changing appetite and poor-quality sleep. You may find yourself getting more colds and illnesses as

YOU

your immune system tries to cope. You probably feel unloved, guilty that you feel like this and doubt that you can do your job. You possibly turn to alcohol or drugs to cope.

If this sounds like you, you need to do something to improve your quality of life and your relationships with those around you. Remember that many people experience this.

These are some of the things you can do for yourself to help yourself? You probably know what to expect if you have been absorbing the information up to this point.

 Get back to a healthy diet. It will give your body access to the nutrition it needs and help your immune system.

Take time for yourself. Get in touch with a friend, either to look after your care recipient or let them take you somewhere to enjoy yourselves. Have fun, laugh and relax.

Practice mindfulness. Even for just ten minutes you will relax your mind and your body, relieve the stress you are feeling and cope better.

Get some exercise. Get to the gym, if you enjoy it. Go to an exercise class, or a swim. Try aquarobics. Or just go for a walk in the fresh air. The endorphins will help.

Get more sleep. Meditation may help with that. Get rid of social media, it doesn't seem to help people sleep!

Get help. Talk to your doctor about how you are feeling and ask for a referral.

 is for

Sleep!

I love this quote from Swanwick Sleep on Pinterest as it describes my sleep habits well!

I want to sleep but my brain won't stop talking to itself.

We know that sleep is important for our health, because we have been told so since we were children. Sleep is good for us because it supports immune and vascular health. Because it supports vascular health, it probably supports brain health too, since we are told that if it's good for the heart, it's good for the brain.

Zzzzzzzz

Sleep is thought to support learning and memory consolidations but scientists in Israel have discovered that sleep is important because it helps restore individual brain cells. In this study, they found individual neurons (and there may be up to 100 billion of them in our brain) performed repair work. As anyone who drives on our roads can tell you, a lot of maintenance is done at night when traffic is much slower, and so the thinking is that this is why we need to sleep. (Applebaum et al., 2019).

Now we know why we need sleep, we need to make sure our habits help us get adequate good quality sleep.

 Exercise is good for sleep if you do it regularly. Leave a few hours before bedtime.

Having a bath may help to relax you and make sleep come more easily.

Avoiding alcohol, caffeine and other stimulants for several hours before bed.

Keep technology in another room from where you sleep. The temptation is to look at it as you lie there waiting to sleep. It helps stimulate your brain, which doesn't help sleep.

Keep to a regular time for bed. A regular sleep pattern helps.

If you can't sleep, don't lie there for long trying to sleep. Get up and do something that is non-stimulating, like reading a book (preferably not an action thriller!)

If all else fails, try something similar to counting sheep. Imagine the skin around your toes. Imagine it surrounding your shin, your knee ... Zzzzzzz

Not the End

We may have reached the end of the alphabet, but it is not the end of Compassionate Communication.

As I wrote this book I realised how widely and deeply compassionate communication goes. I wonder how many alphabet letters you can think that would apply! I'd love to have more examples of 'X' and 'Z'! So, watch this space. There is more to come.

We communicate every day. For most of us, we just do it. For many people their communication has been compromised. Perhaps it's been an accident of birth; perhaps they have never had the freedom to be able to speak their truth. For many, emotional needs inhibit meaningful communication, while for others it is neurological changes that reduce their ability to understand what we say.

NOT THE END

On behalf of everyone who cannot say what they want to say, let's make sure that all our communications arise from compassion.

Thank you

Thank you to all the wonderful people I have taught, educated, worked with and those I've shared stories with about you and your families. I have learnt so much from all of you.

Thank you to the people I will meet, sometimes through cyberspace and often face-to-face as we share what Brain Sparks does. I look forward to joining you on your journey.

Thank you also to my family: my sister Denise, who is my greatest supporter; Andrew and Katy and their families who encourage and help me every step of the way; and to David without whom none of this would be able to happen. I love you all.

Biography

When you are born in Wales, the poem tells us, you are born privileged. Not with a silver spoon in your mouth, but with music in your blood, and with poetry in your soul. In Sue's case, a sense of fun also shines through the serious side of life.

Sue's maternal grandmother had epilepsy and would be institutionalised for long periods at a time, frustrated that people would not listen to what she wanted to say. This is probably the origin of Sue's compassion and support.

After discovering movement and dance in her senior years, Sue became an educator and trainer for the cutting-edge seated movement program, Ageless Grace®, bringing it to Australia in 2012 and New Zealand in 2015. Her energy, spontaneity and sense of fun is enjoyed not just by her grandchildren but the older population she engages with, many of them with cognitive

BIOGRAPHY

challenges. In 2017, Sue brought the AGE-u-cate Training Institute programs to Australia, including the research-based Dementia Live® and Compassionate Touch® programs.

These days, Sue revels in finding ways to empower those caring for our ageing population, including the challenges that dementia brings, through the aged care system, caregivers, and communities. Empty nesters, Sue and her husband are slaves to two ginger cats in Brisbane.

References

Compassionate Touch® and Dementia Live® are research-based training programs developed by the AGE-u-cate Training Institute. Brain Sparks has the licence to use them in Australia, New Zealand and in parts of Asia.

Ageless Grace® is a brain and body health program originating from the US. There are educators who can take classes in many capital cities in Australia as well as trainers who can teach you to become an educator. Ageless Grace® can be found in many countries of the world.

Page iii: Introduction

> Awakenings. In *Wikipedia, The Free Encyclopedia*. Retrieved from https://en.wikipedia.org/w/index.php?title=Awakenings&oldid=885074285

References

Page 2: Brain

Weiss, J. (1952). *Crying at the happy ending.* Retrieved from http://cmtcenter.net/wp-content/uploads/2017/07/Weiss1952.pdf

Page 4: Dementia

Statistics and other information for Australia can be found from Dementia Australia website https://www.dementia.org.au/. Many similar websites are available for other countries

STV News. (2014). Experts make dementia communication breakthrough [Youtube]. Retrieved from https://www.youtube.com/watch?v=MpV7IhhOZ4Y

Page 6: Gratitude

Simple Abundance and Something More. [Website]. Retrieved from http://www.sarahbanbreathnach.com/

Ted. (2013). *The neurons that shaped civilization - VS Ramachandran.* [Youtube]. Retrieved from https://www.youtube.com/watch?v=l80zgw07W4Y

Page 15: Kindness

Australian Kindness Movement. [Website]. Retrieved from http://www.kindness.com.au/

Random Acts of Kindness. [Website].

Retrieved from https://www.randomactsofkindness.org/

Page 18: Non-verbal communication

Knapton, S. (2016). *Dogs understand what we say and how we say it, scientists find.* Retrieved from https://www.telegraph.co.uk/science/2016/08/30/dogs-understand-what-we-say-and-how-we-say-it-scientists-find/

Page 21: Quality of Life

Australian Centre on Quality of Life. [website]

Retrieved from http://www.acqol.com.au/

Page 23: Stigma

SANE Australia. *Supporting the mental health of Australians affected by complex mental illness* [website]

Retrieved from https://www.sane.org/

Page 25: Touch

Romm. C. (2018). *The lasting damage of depriving a child of human touch.*

Retrieved from https://www.thecut.com/2018/06/the-lasting-damage-of-depriving-a-child-of-human-touch.html

References

Page 26: Value

McCarthy, B. (2011). *Hearing the person with dementia: Person-centred approaches to Communication for Families and Caregivers.* Jessica Kingsley Publishers, London.

Page 27: Wellness

World Health Organisation. (2019). *Constitution.*

Retrieved from https://www.who.int/about/who-we-are/constitution

Page 30: Extraordinary

Community Connections Inc. *Extraordinary People.* [Annual Report]. Retrieved from https://www.communityconnectionsinc.org/wp-content/uploads/2012/09/2009-Annual-Report.pdf

Page 32: Sleep

Applebaum, et al. (2019). Sleep increases chromosome dynamics to enable reduction of accumulating DNA damage in single neurons. *Nature Communications* 10 (895). https://doi.org/10.1038/s41467-019-08806-w

'Heads together' icon made by Freepik from www.flaticon.com

How Sue Can Help You

Now that you have read and tried some of the ideas in this book, see how Sue can help you further.

Online courses:

Practical, self-paced for you to work your way through.

- The Compassionate Practice
- The Compassionate Communicator
- The Compassionate Caregiver
- The Compassionate Conversationalist
- The Compassionate Connector

Coach training for those working (or wanting to work) in aged care:

How Sue Can Help You

One or two-day courses either at one of our scheduled training events, via a webinar or by arrangement with your organisation.

- Ageless Grace Educator Certification
- Dementia Live Coach Training
- Compassionate Touch Coach Training

Practitioner Training: Increase your portfolio in aged care

- Dementia Live Coach Training
- Compassionate Touch Coach Training

Scheduled workshop or customised workshops for your organisation.

- Learn what it could be like to live with dementia with the Dementia Live® experience
- Learn techniques to calm and soothe someone you care for, without the need for psychotropic drugs
- Learn how to use memories from the past with your loved one

Conferences and Special Events

Give your conference the "Wow" factor. Let your delegates experience our programs.

- Dementia Live® walk-through

- Compassionate Touch® workshop
- Ageless Grace® energising session

Alternatively ask Sue to speak at your conference.

For more information visit www.brainsparks.com.au

CPSIA information can be obtained
at www.ICGtesting.com
Printed in the USA
LVHW040312100919
630431LV00010B/1307

JOSEPH DIGIACOMO
ADV COM CENTER
VILLANOVA UNIVERSITY
VILLANOVA, PA 19085